Laugh Your Head Off

Great Jokes and Giggles

Mike Artell

Illustration by

Rob Collinet

Sterling Publishing Co., Inc.
New York

Library of Congress Cataloging-in-Publication Data Available

10   1/2012

Published by Sterling Publishing Co., Inc.
387 Park Avenue South, New York, NY 10016
Text © 2006 by Mike Artell
Illustrations © 2006 by Rob Collinet
Distributed in Canada by Sterling Publishing
C/o Canadian Manda Group, 165 Dufferin Street
Toronto, Ontario, Canada M6K 3H6
Distributed in the United Kingdom by GMC Distribution Services
Castle Place, 166 High Street, Lewes, East Sussex, England BN7 1XU
Distributed in Australia by Capricorn Link (Australia) Pty. Ltd.
P.O. Box 704, Windsor, NSW 2756, Australia

Sterling ISBN 13: 978-1-4027-2259-2
        ISBN 10: 1-4027-2259-1

For information about custom editions, special sales, premium and
corporate purchases, please contact Sterling Special Sales
Department at 800-805-5489 or specialsales@sterlingpub.com.

Contents

Doctor, Doctor

Doctor, Doctor, why are you putting a new brain in that man?

He said he wanted to change his mind.

Doctor, Doctor, why did the garbage man leave your office looking so sad?

He's down in the dumps.

Doctor, Doctor, there's an invisible man in the waiting room.
Tell him I can't see him right now.

Doctor, Doctor, I stuck my finger in an electrical outlet.
Young lady, that's shocking!

Doctor, Doctor, a fairy princess is in the waiting room.
That's wand-erful!

Doctor, Doctor, there's an owl in the waiting room.
That's a hoot!

Doctor, Doctor, there's a man with two heads in the waiting room.
Tell him to think twice before coming in here.

Doctor, Doctor, there's a man in the waiting room who wants to use our scale.
Tell him, "no weigh."

Doctor, Doctor, a python wants an appointment.
I'll try to squeeze it in later today.

Doctor, Doctor, there's a boomerang in the waiting room.
Throw it out and tell it to come back later.

Doctor, Doctor, I think I have chicken pox.
Hmmm ... you can scratch that idea.

Doctor, Doctor, a man in the waiting room says he's secretly losing all his hair.

Tell him to keep it under his hat.

Doctor, Doctor, some pigs are bathing in the waiting room.

Hogwash!

Doctor, Doctor, there's a snake in the waiting room and he says he can't swallow.

He probably just has a frog in his throat.

Doctor, Doctor, I have the mumps.

Swell!

Doctor, Doctor, there's a bee in the waiting room.

Tell him to buzz off.

Doctor, Doctor, a mosquito bit me.
Well, go home and bite it back.

Doctor, Doctor, one of my feet is three times bigger than the other.
That's not a foot ... that's a yard!

Doctor, Doctor, people tell me I'm not too bright.
Hold on a minute while I turn on a light.

Doctor, Doctor, people say I tell too many lies.
That's not true!

Doctor, Doctor, I have butterflies in my stomach.
That's what you get for eating caterpillars.

Doctor, Doctor, nobody understands me.
  Huh?

Doctor, Doctor, we have an emergency!
  What is it?
  An elephant with a stuffy nose!

Doctor, Doctor, we have an emergency!
  What is it?
  A giraffe with a sore throat!

Doctor, Doctor, we have an emergency!
  What is it?
  An elephant with a tuskache!

Doctor, Doctor, I have the fly.
  Don't you mean you have the flu?
  No, I ate a fly.

Doctor, Doctor, there's an ape in the waiting room.
  Tell him he needs an ape-pointment.

Doctor, Doctor, a soccer player needs help.
  Good ... I'll get a kick out of that.

Doctor, Doctor, our garbage collector sent us a
postcard!
  How nice ... junk mail!

Doctor, Doctor, why are you putting makeup on that
patient's head?
  I'm trying to help her makeup her mind.

Doctor, Doctor, can you cure my pet whale?
No ... just leave whale enough alone.

Doctor, Doctor, my foot hurts.
Step on it ... I'm very busy.

Doctor, Doctor, I refuse to tell you what my problem is.
You don't say.

Doctor, Doctor, a goat is having babies in the waiting room.
That goat must be kidding!

Doctor, Doctor, are you doing brain surgery on yourself?
I sure am; I'm going to give you a piece of my mind.

Doctor, Doctor, there's a ghost in the waiting room.
Yes, I know. He has a boo-boo.

Doctor, Doctor, there's a sick magician in the waiting room.
Tell him I can't see him until he gets his act together.

Doctor, Doctor, there's a ballerina in the waiting room.
Well, tell her to stay on her toes.

Doctor, Doctor, there's a crazy astronaut in the waiting room.
He's not crazy, he's just spaced-out.

Doctor, Doctor, there's a barber in the waiting room.
That's guy's starting to get in my hair.

Doctor, Doctor, there's a very rich man in the waiting room.
I'll bet he feels like a million dollars.

Doctor, Doctor, there's a tightrope walker on the phone.
Tell him I'm on another line.

Doctor, Doctor, there's a sick rabbit in the waiting room.
I know. It's having a bad hare day.

Doctor, Doctor, why are you tickling your patient?
  Because laughter is the best medicine.

Doctor, Doctor, I have a sore throat.
  Gee, what a pain in the neck.

Doctor, Doctor, I dreamed I was an acorn and a pecan.
  You must be nuts.

Doctor, Doctor, what did that man say when you told him you needed to remove his appendix?
  He thought I was kidding and told me to cut it out.

Doctor, Doctor, that man said you didn't like his intestines.
  No. I said I hated his guts.

Doctor, Doctor, there's a snowman in the waiting room.
  Tell him not to lose his cool.

Doctor, Doctor, there's a gingerbread man in the waiting room.
  That guy is flaky, but ask him if he has any dough.

Doctor, Doctor, there's an opossum in the waiting room.
  Tell it to hang loose for a while.

Doctor, Doctor, there's a soccer player in the waiting room.
  Kick him out of here!

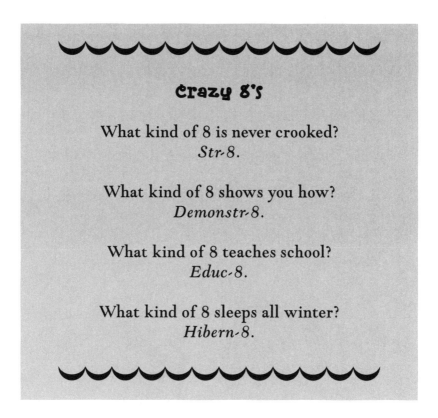

Crazy 8's

What kind of 8 is never crooked?
Str-8.

What kind of 8 shows you how?
Demonstr-8.

What kind of 8 teaches school?
Educ-8.

What kind of 8 sleeps all winter?
Hibern-8.

Doctor, Doctor, Max Smith, Max Jones, and Max Davis are waiting to see you.
Tell them I'm Maxed-out.

Doctor, Doctor, there's an upset surfer who wants to see you.
Doggone it! Those guys are always making waves.

Doctor, Doctor, there's a lady out here putting lipstick on her head.
Hmmm ... Sounds like she's trying to make up her mind.

Doctor, Doctor, it's minus five degrees in this waiting room!

Don't be so negative.

Doctor, Doctor, did that football player borrow 25 cents from you?

Yes, but he never gave me my quarterback.

Doctor, Doctor, there's a mountain climber in the waiting room.

Tell her to take a hike.

Criss-Cross Critters

What do you get if you cross a hummingbird and a turkey?

A very skimpy Thanksgiving dinner.

What do you get if you cross a shark and a hyena?

An animal that bites you and then laughs about it.

What do you get if you cross a cricket with a centipede?

I'm not sure, but when it rubs its legs together, it's incredibly noisy!

What do you get if you cross a beaver with a termite?

An animal that chops down a tree then eats the whole thing.

What do you get if you cross a bear with a rooster?

An animal that hibernates, then wakes itself up in the morning.

What do you get if you cross a migrating bird, a pack rat and an elephant?

An animal that packs its own trunk before it flies south for the winter.

What do you get if you cross cows and rattlesnakes?

Rattled cattle.

What do you get if you cross Godzilla with a bee?

A bumble-beast.

What do you get if you cross a laptop with a skunk?

A com-pew-ter.

What do you get if you cross a whale with a parrot?

A blubber-mouth.

What do you get if you cross a giraffe with an ostrich?

An animal that can stick its head 10 feet underground.

What do you get if you cross a swamp reptile with a teacher?

An alli-grader.

What do you get if you cross a cow with a duck?

Milk and quackers.

What do you get if you cross a poodle with a fly?

A dog and French flies.

What do you get if you cross a chameleon and a camel?

Camel-flage.

What do you get if you cross a squirrel with a monkey?

An animal that stores bananas for the winter.

What do you get if you cross a hummingbird with a T-Rex?

A tiny-saur.

What do you get if you cross a platypus with a beaver?

An animal that's flat on both ends.

What do you get if you cross a swordfish with a bumblebee?

An animal that's pointed on both ends.

What do you get if you cross an owl with a fish?

An animal that can see really well underwater at night.

What do you get if you cross a fish with some Dutch cheese?

A barra-Gouda.

What do you get if you cross a hummingbird with a fly?

A humbug.

What do you get if you cross a python and an orange?

A fruit that squeezes its own juice.

What do you get if you cross a dolphin and a shark?

A dork.

What do you get if you cross a lion and a drummer?
The King of Beats.

What do you get if you cross a boulder and a biscuit?
Rock and roll.

What do you get if you cross an electric eel and a light bulb?
A lamp.

What do you get if you cross a woodpecker, an owl, and a laughing hyena?

 An *animal that says:*
   "Knock, knock.
     "Who?
   "Ha ha ha!"

What do you get if you cross a dollar bill with a kangaroo?

 A *buckaroo.*

What do you get if you cross a pecan and a lobster?

 A *nut that can crack itself open.*

Hee-Hee—Rhyme Three

What do you call ...
A place to keep money, what pirates make you walk,
and what a dentist does when she pulls your tooth?
  Bank, plank, yank.

What do you call ...
Something horses eat, what skunks do with their odor, and what you should do when you parents tell you something?

Hay, spray, obey.

What do you call ...
The place where you sleep, string that you sew with, and toast before it's toasted?

Bed, thread, bread.

What do you call ...
The football player that makes extra points, how you feel when you get the flu, and an alarm clock?

Kicker, sicker, ticker.

What do you call ...
An animal that digs underground, a baby horse, and
money you pay to cross a bridge?
    Mole, foal, toll.

What do you call ...
A large animal with antlers, a kind of evergreen tree,
and a bird that migrates?
    Moose, spruce, goose.

What do you call ...
What cowboys wear on each foot, what owls do, and a
kind of salamander?
    Boot, hoot, newt.

What do you call ...
A large fancy boat, what you do to a fly, and a
common name for a dog?
    Yacht, swat, Spot.

What do you call ...
The red liquid in your veins, a mixture of water and
dirt, and a slang expression for a potato?
    Blood, mud, spud.

What do you call ...
A bird's home, a quiz, and your little brother?
    Nest, test, pest.

What do you call ...
What keeps your belt closed, a joke, and a finger joint?
    Buckle, chuckle, knuckle.

What do you call ...
A shape with four equal sides, an animal that
hibernates, and the stuff on top of your head?
  Square, bear, hair.

What do you call ...
A purple fruit, an animal that eats bananas, and sticky
stuff that you tear off a roll?
  Grape, ape, tape.

What do you call ...
The top of a mountain, a bird's mouth, and the sound
a mouse makes?
  Peak, beak, squeak.

What do you call ...
A forest animal, a place to dock a boat, and 365 days?
  Deer, pier, year.

What do you call ...
A mother chicken, Chinese money, and a bear's home?
  Hen, yen, den.

What do you call ...
A man who's getting married, a flower that's about to
open, and a grave?
  Groom, bloom, tomb.

What do you call ...
A bird that migrates, good fortune, and cafeteria
food?
  Duck, luck, yuck.

What do you call ...
A windy day, someone with a cold, and a pizza?
  Breezy, sneezy, cheesy.

What do you call ...
Fake hair, a hog, and a small branch?
  Wig, pig, twig.

What do you call ...
A vehicle with two wheels, a long walk, and a big nail?
  Bike, hike, spike.

What do you call ...
A biblical boat, a man-eating fish, and a place to play?
  Ark, shark, park.

What do you call ...
What you fish with, when a boy and girl go out together, how heavy you are

Bait, date, weight.

What do you call ...
Something you study for, the part of your body where your lungs are, the opposite of east.

Test, chest, west.

What do you call ...
The thing on a camel's back, what you use to inflate your bicycle tire, and what's left after you cut down a tree?

Hump, pump, stump.

Little Bratley

Bratley! Why didn't you answer the phone?
I would have, Mom, but it didn't ask me anything.

Bratley, you're late for school again today.
Actually, I'm just really early for school tomorrow.

TEACHER: Bratley, where is your homework?
BRATLEY: My dog ate it.
TEACHER: That's terrible!
BRATLEY: That's what my dog said.

MOM: Bratley, when will you ever learn?
BRATLEY: That's what my teacher wants to know.

MOM: Bratley, you're going to give me a headache.
BRATLEY: Wow, Mom, I didn't know you could tell the future!

MOM: Bratley! What are all these French fries doing on the sofa?
BRATLEY: It's okay, Mom. They're couch potatoes!

DAD: Bratley, you got an A, a B, a C, a D, and an F on this report card.
BRATLEY: Yeah Dad, I know. I'm hoping to get the rest of the alphabet on my next report card.

MOM: Bratley, your hair is a perfect mess!
BRATLEY: Wow! You really think it's PERFECT? Thanks!

MOM: Bratley, you're driving me crazy!
BRATLEY: Gee, Mom, I thought I was too young to drive.

MOM: Bratley, your bedroom is an absolute disaster.
BRATLEY: I know, but you should have seen it before I cleaned it up.

BRATLEY: Hey Mom, did you know there are four new states?

MOM: Are you sure?

BRATLEY: Yep ... New Mexico, New York, New Jersey, and New Hampshire

MOM: Bratley, I think you're playing too many video games?

BRATLEY: Why do you say that?

MOM: Because you keep trying to "pause" your sister.

MOM: Bratley, you're the messiest kid in the world!

BRATLEY: Wow, Mom, you've met EVERY other kid in the world?

MOM: Bratley, if you keep this up, you're going to make me lose my mind.
BRATLEY: That's okay, Mom. If you lose it, I'll help you look for it.

MOM: Bratley, how many times have I told you to sit up straight?
BRATLEY: Whoa, Mom, I don't know. I'm not too good at math.

MOM: Bratley, why don't you use your manners?
BRATLEY: Gee, Mom, I'm afraid if I use them, I'll run out, and then I'll need more.

BRATLEY: Hey, Mom, did you know I'm a magician?
MOM: Really? Can you do any magic tricks?
BRATLEY: Sure! I can make a bowl of ice cream disappear.

MOM: These batteries are running low.
BRATLEY: Cool! Let me look ... I've never seen batteries run before.

BRATLEY: Mom do I really need to take a bath?
MOM: I don't know ... let's ask those flies that are circling around you.

DAD: Why are you pushing your bedroom wall?
BRATLEY: Mom asked me to straighten my room.

TEACHER: Bratley, do you know, "Mary had a little lamb?"
BRATLEY: Sure, but that's nothin'. When my mom saw my report card, she had a cow.

TEACHER: When was America founded?
BRATLEY: I didn't even know it was losted.

TEACHER: Why is your computer so cold?
BRATLEY: Because I'm on the Winter-net.

MOM: What would you like on your pizza?
BRATLEY: My mouth!

TEACHER: Have you ever flown on an airplane?
BRATLEY: Nope. But I've flown *in* one.

TEACHER: Can anyone in the class tell me what do you get if you multiply 13 times 14 and divide the result by 7?
BRATLEY: You get confused!

BRATLEY: Dad! There's something behind this door going, "squeak, squeak!"
DAD: Is it a mouse?
BRATLEY: Nope, it's a rusty hinge.

TEACHER: Bratley, when did Columbus discover America?
BRATLEY: When his boat hit the shore.

MUSIC TEACHER: Bratley, why are you rubbing that guitar against your head?
BRATLEY: I'm trying to learn to play by ear.

DAD: What do you want to be when you grow up, Bratley?
BRATLEY: An adult.

BRATLEY: Dad, I put this seashell up to my ear and I heard something!
DAD: Was it the ocean?
BRATLEY: No, I heard a crab say, "Put me down!"

BRATLEY: Dad, I need the keys to the car.
DAD: What?! You're too young to get behind the wheel of a car.
BRATLEY: Well, Mom just told me I'm driving her up a wall.

MOM: Hurry or you'll miss the school bus!
BRATLEY: Gee, Mom, the school bus left me yesterday, and I didn't miss it at all.

MOM: Eat your veggies. They'll make you big and strong.
BRATLEY: Are you sure? Rabbits look pretty wimpy to me.

DAD: I wonder what's causing all this traffic?
BRATLEY: Hmmm ... it might be all those cars.

Calendar Crack-ups

What month is the most tired?
Janu-WEARY.

In what months is it okay to tell a lie?
In FIB-ruary and Ju-LIE.

What month always asks permission?
May.

What month do woodcutters like best?
Sep-TIMBER!

What month do Brazilian dancers like best?
De-SAMBA.

Knock-knocks

Knock, knock!
  Who's there?
Anita
  Anita who?
Anita clean up my room before I can go outside.

Knock, knock!
Who's there?
Bailey
Bailey who?
Bailey half the ice cream is left. Who ate it?

Knock, knock!
Who's there?
Beth
Beth who?
Beth things come in small packages.

Knock, knock!
Who's there?
Carey
Carey who?
Carey these groceries for me.

Knock, knock!
Who's there?
Carla
Carla who?
Carla on the phone and
ask her for a date.

Knock, knock!
Who's there?
Celeste
Celeste who?
Celeste piece of pie.
Want to share it?

Knock, knock!
Who's there?
Dawn
Dawn who?
Dawn go outside,
it's raining.

Knock, knock!
Who's there?
Dustin
Dustin who?
Dustin the furniture will
make it shine.

Knock, knock!
Who's there?
Eden
Eden who?
Eden all your vegetables
will make you healthy.

Knock, knock!
Who's there?
Harry
Harry who?
Harry up and open the
door! There's a dog
chasing me!

Knock, knock!
Who's there?
Holt
Holt who?
Holt on a minute and I'll
tell you.

Knock, knock!
Who's there?
Howard
Howard who?
Howard you like me to
fix your doorbell?

Knock, knock!
Who's there?
Imogene.
Imogene who?
Imogene pocket I found
a five dollar bill.

Knock, knock!
Who's there?
Jake
Jake who?
Jake, rattle, and roll!

Knock, knock!
Who's there?
Josh
Josh who?
Josh wanted to see if you would say,
"Who's there?"

Knock, knock!
Who's there?
Juan
Juan who?
Juan to come outside and play?

Knock, knock!
   Who's there?
Kent
   Kent who?
Kent come in, sorry.

                    Knock, knock!
                       Who's there?
                    Jill
                       Jill who?
                    Jill out! You're too tense.

Knock, knock!
   Who's there?
Lorraine
   Lorraine who?
Lorraine in Spain stays mainly on the plain.

Knock, knock!
  Who's there?
Murray
  Murray who?
Murray me ... I love you!

Knock, knock!
  Who's there?
Noah
  Noah who?
Noah mount of money could convince me.

Knock, knock!
  Who's there?
Owen
  Owen who?
Owen people money can get you in a lot of trouble.

Knock, knock!
Who's there?
Phillip.
Phillip who?
Phillip the pool with
water, I wanna go
swimming!

Knock, knock!
Who's there?
Sadie
Sadie who?
Sadie alphabet
from A to Z

Knock, knock!
Who's there?
Ridge
Ridge who?
Ridge people have lots of
money.

Knock, knock!
Who's there?
Shay
Shay who?
Shay whatever you want
to shay.

Knock, knock!
Who's there?
Rye
Rye who?
Rye are you giving me so
much trouble?

Knock, knock!
Who's there?
Soren
Soren who?
Soren wood makes a lotta
sawdust.

41

Knock, knock!
    Who's there?
Talon
    Talon who?
Talon lies is a very bad thing to do.

Knock, knock!
    Who's there?
Tanner
    Tanner who?
Tanner fifteen years from now,
I'll be all grown up.

Knock, knock!
    Who's there?
Toby
    Toby who?
Toby or not Toby,
that is the question.

Knock, knock!
    Who's there?
Troy
    Troy who?
Troy opening up the door and
finding out!

Knock, knock!
Who's there?
Van
Van who?
Van are you coming over to see me?

Knock, knock!
Who's there?
Wade
Wade who?
Wade just a minute ... not so fast!

Knock, knock!
Who's there?
Warner.
Warner who?
Warner go outside and play soccer?

Knock, knock!
  Who's there?
Wendy
  Wendy who?
Wendy clock strikes twelve,
you'd better be home.

          Knock, knock, knock, knock, knock,
          knock, knock, knock!
            Who's there?
          An octopus!

What's the Difference?

What's the difference between adolescent fashion garments and feet that have just been washed?

One is teen clothes and the other is clean toes.

What's the difference between beef jerky and a man with sunburn?

One is dried food and the other is a fried dude.

What's the difference between a weekend movie and an insect in spring?

One is a matinee and the other is a gnat in May.

What's the difference between a rude person and angry flags?

One has bad manners and the others are mad banners.

What's the difference between a clown and someone who loves dollar bills?

One is a funny man and the other is a money fan.

Frozen Funnies

Where do people at the North Pole get their
haircut?
At the brrr-brrr shop.

What's the coldest tropical island?
Brrrr-muda.

What kind of animals are penguins?
Brrrrr-ds.

What kind of criminals do they have at the
North Pole?
Brrrr-gulars.

What's the difference between Asian eating utensils
and a fence around a chicken coop?
One is chopsticks and the other stops chicks.

What's the difference between a short rest and a hat
for a bug?
One is a catnap and the other is a gnat cap.

What's the difference between a rulebook and a
statue?
One is a master plan and the other is a plaster man.

What's the difference between a squashed candy and bad handwriting?

One is a pressed mint and the other is messed print.

What's the difference between what a barber gives you and a hospital in the jungle?

One is a haircut and the other is a care hut.

What's the difference between a container for a noontime meal and ten padlocks?

One is a lunch box and the other is a bunch of locks.

What's the difference between a rope tied snugly and a baby who lives in a castle?

One is a tight knot and the other is a knight's tot.

Hen humor

Where does a hen keep her wallet?
In her hen-bag.

How does a hen steer her bicycle?
With the hen-dlebars.

Why did the teacher give the little hen a bad grade?
Because she had bad hen-dwriting.

What does a hen wear in prison?
Hen-cuffs.

What kind of Mexican food do hens like?
Hen-chiladas.

Why did everyone go hear the little hen sing?
Because she was very hen-tertaining.

What's the difference between the exhaust tube on a car and someone who sunburns easily?
One is a tail pipe, the other is a pale type.

What's the difference between a man with no hair and a hiker carrying a sleeping bag?
One is a bald head and the other is a hauled bed.

What's the difference between very cold toes and ears and being scared of the person you work for?

One is frostbite, the other is boss fright.

What's the difference between a small, nectar-eating bird and a bunch of cows standing around doing nothing?

One is a hummingbird, the other is a bumming herd.

What's the difference between a nasty insect and someone who helps musical groups perform better?

One is a cockroach, the other is a rock coach.

What's the difference between the ocean and a fish market?

In the ocean, the scales are on the fish. In a fish market, the fish are on the scales.

Chop a Letter

How do you transform the sound a wolf makes into a bird that comes out at night?

Chop the "h" from howl *and make it* owl.

How do you transform cleaning something into what's left after a fire?

Chop the "w" from wash *and make it* ash.

How do you transform cutting the fleece off a sheep into what your ear does?

Chop the "s" from shear *and make it* hear.

How do you transform a small store into the way a frog moves?

Chop the "s" from shop *and make it* hop.

How do you transform a ten-cent coin into low light?
Chop the "e" from dime *and make it* dim.

How do you transform creating pictures with a pencil into uncooked food?

Chop the "d" from draw *and make it* raw.

How do you transform a pointed stick into a fruit?
  Chop the "s" from spear *and make it a* pear.

How do you transform a locomotive into water falling from the sky?
  Chop the "t" from train *and make it* rain.

How do you transform a piece of furniture into something you comb?
  Chop the "c" from chair *and make it* hair.

How do you transform not in this place into this place?
  Chop the "t" from there *and make it* here.

How do you transform pushing a broom into what you do when you're very sad?
  Chop the "s" from sweep *and make it* weep.

How do you transform an item of clothing that superheroes wear into a kind of hat?
  Chop the "e" from cape *and make it* cap.

How do you transform a word that means "to hold tightly" into a quick breath?
  Chop the "r" from grasp *and make it* gasp.

How do you transform a design into a skillet?
  Chop the "l" from plan *and make it* pan.

How do you transform a word that means "to perspire" into a place to rest?
  Chop the "w" from sweat *and make it* seat.

How do you transform a word that means chubby into something you use to blow up a ball?

Chop the "l" from plump *and make it* pump.

How to you make a word that means to get smaller into a place to wash dishes?

Chop the "hr" from shrink *and make it* sink.

How do you transform small rocks into a place to bury someone?

Chop the "l" from gravel *and make it a* grave.

How do you transform the opposite of hot into the opposite of young?

Chop the "c" from cold *and make it* old.

How do you transform a water vessel into a snake?

Chop the "t" from boat *and make it* boa.

How do you transform something you sit on into a large body of water?

Chop the "t" from seat *and make it* sea.

How do you transform hitting a drum into what you do at mealtime?

Chop the "b" from beat *and make it* eat.

How do you transform fear into the opposite of left?

Chop the "f" from fright *and make it* right.

How do you transform a distant sun into black, oily goop?

Chop the "s" from star *and make it* tar.

How do you transform what you put food on into tardiness?

Chop the "p" from plate *and make it* late.

How do you transform a place where cows live into the body part that lifts your hand?

Chop the "f" from farm *and make it* arm.

How do you transform an aircraft into a strategy?

Chop the "e" from plane *and make it* plan.

How do you transform extreme fear into a mistake?

Chop the "t" from terror *and make it* error.

How do you transform what comes out of your eyes when you cry into what you hear with?

Chop the "t" from tears *and make it* ears.

How do you transform what a leaky faucet does into tearing a piece of cloth?

Chop the "d" from drip *and make it* rip.

How do you transform a covering for your face into what you do when you pose a question?

Chop the "m" from mask *and make it* ask.

How do you transform what the doctor gives you with a needle into the opposite of cold?

Chop the "s" from shot *and make it* hot.

How do you transform something a dentist fixes into the sound a horn makes?

Chop the "h" from tooth *and make it* toot.

How do you transform a group of sheep into something that keeps a door closed?

Chop the "f" from flock *and make it* lock.

How do you transform the earth you stand on into something circular?

Chop the "g" from ground *and make it* round.

How do you transform a leap in the air into a baseball official?

Chop the "j" from jump *and make it* ump.

Have you Ever Seen...

A FISH BOWL?

A COW POKE?

A MILK SHAKE?

A POLE VAULT?

A SQUARE DANCE?

AN EGG PLANT?

A T PARTY?

A LETTER BOX?

A DOOR STEP?

AN EAR RING?

A NET WORK?

A FRUIT FLY?

How do you transform a cardboard container into a large bovine animal?

Chop the "b" from box *and make it* ox.

How do you transform a stringed musical instrument into a place where prisoners stay?

Chop the "o" from cello *and make it a* cell.

Sounds the same

What is a walkway on an island?
An isle aisle.

What do you call money hidden in a secret place?
A cash cache.

What do you call the reason blackbirds make lots of noise?

The caws' cause.

What do you call the location of your eye?

Your sight site.

What do you call a black mineral that miners dig from the ground in winter?

Cold coal.

What do you call a rough and bumpy road or pathway?

A coarse course.

What do you call a military officer's corn seeds?

The colonel's kernels.

What do you call the place where a physician keeps his boat?

The doc's dock.

What do female deer do when they get very tired?

The does doze.

What do you call it when two different pairs of people are sword fighting?

Dual duels.

What do you get when you tighten the ropes on tents too much?

You get tense tents.

What does a person from Thailand wear around his neck?

A *Thai tie*.

What do you do when you hit a seashell with a stick?

You conk a conch.

What do you do when you bend little tiny specks of something?

You flex the flecks.

What do you do when you listen at this place?

You hear here.

What do you call the noise that tennis players make?
  Racquet racket.

What do you call a group of musicians that are
forbidden to play?
  A banned band.

What do you call a very strange marketplace?
  A bizarre bazaar.

What do you call a smashed purple vegetable?
  A beat beet.

What do fleas on dogs do when you spray them with bug spray?
The fleas flee.

What happens to shellfish that work out in a gym for long periods of time?
The mussels get muscles.

What do you call a sailor's bellybutton?
A naval navel.

What is a wonderful drain cover?
A great grate.

What is bunny fur?
Hare hair.

What happened when the cowboy called the cows?
The herd heard.

What kind of song do men sing in church?
A him hymn.

What did the runner have when he couldn't finish the race?
A laps lapse.

What do you call a funeral for a small fruit?
A berry bury.

What probably happened if your car won't stop?
A brake break.

What do you call an underground home for a donkey?
A burro burrow.

What do you call an ordinary aircraft?
A plain plane.

What do you call a line of fish eggs?
A roe row.

What does a button do?
Close clothes.

What do you call nice woodland animals?
Dear deer.

When is a cow picky?
When it wants to choose what it chews.

What happens when you surf the Internet?
You catch sight of a site.

What do you call a group of crickets that hang out together?
A click clique.

What do people who work on boats do when they're out at sea?
The crews cruise.

What do deer use to make bread?
Doe dough.

What happened when the bear scratched its back on the tree?

It left fur on the fir.

What do you call a duck that never bathes?

A foul fowl.

What is a reasonable amount of money to pay for an airplane ticket?

A fair fare.

What kind of boat does a pixie use to cross the river?
A *fairy ferry*.

What is an electric bulb that doesn't weigh very much?
A *light light*.

Weird Widdles

Do monsters have good table manners?
  No, they're always "goblin" their food.

What is a sleepy king's favorite Christmas carol?
  Silent Knight.

How do little ghouls get to school?
In monster trucks.

What do little boy monsters become when they grow up?
Mansters.

Where do most monsters live?
In Growly-fornia.

What is the scariest underwater monster?
Codzilla.

What do knights wear when they go to sleep?
Knight gowns.

What holiday do monsters like best?
Fangs-giving.

What monsters are afraid of small spaces?
Those with claws-trophobia.

What kind of monster keeps getting lost?
A where wolf.

What do knights do when they get scared?
They turn on the knight light.

Who is the grossest monster?
Frankenslime.

Where do knights go to dance?
To a knight club.

What do teenage monsters say when they like something?

They say, "That's very ghoul!"

How does a dentist remove a vampire's fangs?

With vampliers.

How do you know if a monster is sleeping under your bed?

When the monster sleepwalks, you and your bed go sleepwalking too.

Who keeps an eye on all the knights?

The knight watchman.

What's a monster's favorite cheese?
  Muenster.

What's a monster's favorite month?
  Oct-ogre.

What's your little baby monster's name?
  Gus. It's short for Disgusting.

What would you have named it if it had been a girl?
  Belle. It's short for Horri-Belle.

What is the weirdest vegetable?
  The human bean.

What kind of birds do knights like best?
Knightingales.

What animal is big, gray, and wears glass slippers?
Cinderelliphant.

Why did one Cyclops get along so well with the other?
They saw everything eye-to-eye.

Which zombie won the weird zombie race?
None of them ... it was dead even.

Why did the two-headed monster win every race?
Because he always had a head start.

What fairy tale monster lost her sheep?
Little Bo Creep.

Do you think the gingerbread man is weird?
Well, he does seem a little flaky.

Why didn't the little skeleton do his homework?
Because he was a lazy bones.

ZOMBIE MOM #1: My, your little zombie is getting big.
ZOMBIE MOM #2: Yes, he's already in first grave.

Who brings candy to all the good little skeletons?
The Easter Boney.

What did the old monster say to the young monster?
My, how you've groaned!

Which do space monsters prefer, thin hamburgers or thick ones?
They prefer the meteor (meatier) ones.

Where do ghosts mail their letters?
At the ghost office.

Do vampires make mistakes?
No, but ghosts make boo-boos!

Who is the worst entertainer in the Himalayan mountains?
The Abominable Showman.

Do ghosts hunt with guns?
No, they use a boo and arrow.

Sunken Silliness

What is a fish's favorite country?
Fin-land.

Who do fish see when they don't feel well?
A doctorpus.

GIRL #1: What's wrong?
GIRL #2: I took my pet for a walk and it died.
GIRL #1: That's too bad. What kind of pet was it?
GIRL #2: A goldfish.

What fish smells the worst?
  The stink-ray.

What was the wise old fish's favorite saying?
  All's whale that ends whale.

What fish is the most spiritual?
  The holy mackerel.

A bunch of bull

What kind of bull is the cutest?
Adora-bull.

What kind of bull gets along best with others?
Agreea-bull.

What kind of bull do you have to put together?
Assem-bull.

What kind of bull can you always trust?
Believa-bull.

What kind of bull is hard to see?
Invisi-bull.

What's purple and white, lives in the sea, and has big teeth?
The grape white shark.

MOTHER FISH: Junior, hurry up, you're going to be late for school!
LITTLE FISH: Okay, Mom, I'll be there in just a minnow.

What kind of lions are the best swimmers?
Sea lions.

75

Why don't oysters share their toys?
Because they're shellfish.

Did you like that book about sharks?
No, it seemed a little fishy to me.

How do oysters communicate?
They talk on their shell-phones.

Why did the angry sailor walk strangely?
Because he had a ship on his shoulder.

CAPTAIN: Sailor, I want you to get some new glasses.
SAILOR: Eye, eye, sir.

What kind of chips do sailors like best?
Battle-chips.

Did you catch any stinging fish when you went to the beach?
I didn't catch any fish, but I caught some "rays."

Animal Antics

What did the mother bee say to the bad baby bee?
  Beehive yourself!

What constellation do baby hogs like best?
  The Pig Dipper.

Why didn't the baby goose like his blanket?
Because it was a hand-me-"down."

Where do pigs park their cars?
In a pork-ing lot.

Which state is like a horse's hair?
Maine.

Why didn't the pig get invited to any parties?
Because he was a boar.

What kind of anteater has the prettiest yard?
The yard-vark.

What black and white animal that can't fly would you see near the water?
   A panda on vacation.

How do cows communicate?
   They talk on their moo-bile phones.

When is the best time to find frogs?
   During leap year.

What month do pigs like best?
   HOG-*ust.*

What month do cattle like best?
   OX-*tober.*

Why did the poodle go to bed early?
   Because it was dog tired.

What do you call a sheep that makes pancakes for breakfast?
   A "battering" ram.

What kind of music do rabbits like best?
   Hip Hop.

What kind of deer is the scariest?
   The cari-boo!

FATHER GLOWWORM: I'm worried about our son.
MOTHER GLOWWORM: Why?
FATHER GLOWWORM: I don't think he's too bright.

Why do bears get so many splinters?
Because they walk around bear-foot.

What's the opposite of a cool cat?
A hot dog.

What dinosaurs have the most auto accidents?
T-Wrecks.

GIRL #1: I'm worried about my dog.
GIRL #2: Why?
GIRL #1: Because he keeps getting into fights.
GIRL #2: What kind of dog is he?
GIRL #1: A boxer.

Where do insects shop?
At flea markets.

Which insect knows the most about computers?
The inter-gnat.

What's huge, gray, and bounces?
An elephant that's bungee jumping.

Are balloon animals smart?
No, they're airheads.

How do apes lock their homes?
With mon-keys.

What insect is the best musician?
The horn-et.

What do rodents use to keep their breath fresh?
  Mousewash.

How do hogs clean their teeth?
  With tooth-pigs.

Why do giraffes have such long necks?
  Because their heads are so far from their bodies.

What dogs make the best scientists?
  Labs.

What dogs are the best at telling time?
  Clock-er spaniels.

Crazy Cans

What kind of can has feathers and a big beak?
A peli-can.

What kind of can looks like a real person?
A manni-can.

What kind of can lives in the rain forest?
A tou-can.

What kind of can is a real nut?
A pe-can.

What happens when dinosaurs drive cars?
Tyrannosaurus wrecks.

What game do baby cows like best?
Peek-a-moo.

What goes, "Thhh, thhh?"
A snake with a lisp.

How did the police find out who robbed Old
MacDonald?
The pig squealed and the mouse ratted.

Where do horses live?
  In a neigh-borhood.

What dog whines the most?
  The Chi-waaa-waaa.

What is the fastest land animal?
  A gorilla on a motorcycle.

What animal has big ears and eats carrots?
  An elephant on a diet.

MOM MOUSE: Did you take a bath?
LITTLE MOUSE: Yes, and I'm squeaky clean.

Why do bats fly at night?
Because they don't know how to drive.

What is the most excited jungle animal?
The hyper-potamus.

What swings on a vine and has black and white stripes?
A chimpanzebra.

Just Plain Goofy

What bread has the worst attitude?
  Sour-dough.

What's the weirdest food?
  Wacky-roni

What did the baker get when he put dynamite in the dough?
  Fire-crackers.

Why was the little peanut punished?
Because he made his parents nuts.

FATHER CARROT: Junior ... what are you doing?
JUNIOR CARROT: Vegging out.
FATHER CARROT: Good boy!

What kind of toes do you find underground?
Pota-toes.

What do you call a banana split that falls to the ground?
A banana splat.

Tom Swifties

"The money's in this big steel box," he said safely.

"Go to the back of the boat," the captain said sternly.

"Give me the knife," she said sharply.

"I think these are my underwear," he said briefly.

"The brain is missing," the scientist said absentmindedly.

What kind of table is good to eat?
   A *vege-table*.

What kind of vegetables do drummers like best?
   Beets.

What kind of nail should you never hit with a hammer?
   Your fingernail.

What nursery rhyme character fell off the wall and into a trash can?
   Humpty Dumpster.

Is the pest-control man nervous?
No, he's just a little "antsy."

Why did the silly girl put clothes on her letter?
Because the postman said it needed a name and a dress.

Where is the best place to find a fan in the middle of the summer?
In a baseball stadium.

When is it all right to steal something?
When you're playing baseball and can steal a base.

What is something black and red that people jump on?
A checkerboard.

What kind of ring is always square?
A boxing ring.

Last Laugh

GIRL: Why are you giving your bees away?
BEEKEEPER: They're free-bees.

What is the first thing little goats learn in school?
  The alpha-butt.

Did you hear about the bearded barber that was almost hit by a car?
He had a very close shave.

Why do pilots sit in the front of the plane?
Because there's no room to lie down.

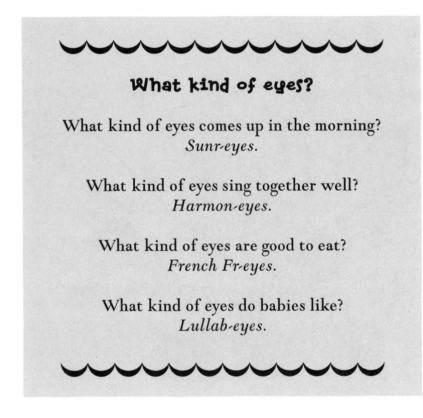

What kind of eyes?

What kind of eyes comes up in the morning?
Sunr-eyes.

What kind of eyes sing together well?
Harmon-eyes.

What kind of eyes are good to eat?
French Fr-eyes.

What kind of eyes do babies like?
Lullab-eyes.

What do you call a genius with a bad memory?
A knew-it-all.

In what city are people the most timid?
Shy-enne, Wyoming.

What city never stays in the same place?
Rome.

Did you get a cold when you went to Hawaii?
No, I got a hula-hooping cough.

What goes from city to city but never moves?
A road.

What kind of plant hates to have company?
The Be-gone-ya.

What is the sleepiest planet?
Nap-tune.

Why did the little gnome hate school?
His teacher gave him too much gnome-work.

What two pupils do teachers see every day?
The ones in their eyes.

What part of a mountain hears the best?
The mountain-ears.

What smells but has no smell?
Your nose.

KID #1: Last night I caught a mouse behind my house.
KID #2: That's nothing. This morning I caught a school bus in front of my house.

What did the math teacher's clock say?
Arithme-tick, arithme-tock, arithme-tick, arithme-tock.

What kind of game can you play with nine clocks and your feet?
Tick Tock Toe.

What says, "Atchoo-choo-choo?"
A train with a head cold.

What kind of cap does everyone wear, but never on their heads?
A kneecap.

What has two arms, two legs, and a horn?
A trumpet player.

What did the Hip Hop singer want for his birthday?
It didn't matter as long as it was rapped.

Did they catch the burglar who stole the piano?
Yes, and now he's got to face the music.

What musical instrument do bank robbers like best?
The lute.

Do choirs like to sing?
Of chorus!

How do you say goodbye to your spaghetti?
Hasta la pasta.

Why is saying goodbye like watching a centipede?
*Because one is "so long" and the other is s-o-o-o-o-o
long.*

Why is a car salesman like someone going away?
One says, "Buy! Buy!" and the other says, "Bye-bye."

How do you say goodbye to an ape?
"See you soon, you baboon."

How do you say goodbye to a snake?
"If that rattle's showin', I gotta be goin'."

How do you say goodbye to a buoy?
"Bye buoy."

How do you say goodbye at the end of a book?
"I hate to be rude, but I'm outta here, dude."

About the Author

Mike Artell lives in Covington, Louisiana, which is near New Orleans. Mike has written and illustrated dozens of picture books, science books, drawing books, and humor books. Many of Mike's books have won awards. Each year, Mike visits more than 50 schools where he shows kids (and teachers!) how to think, write and draw more creatively.

To learn more about Mike's books, videos, and personal appearances, visit www.mikeartell.com.

Index